DOUBLE Trouble

Written by Dominic Barker
Illustrated by Paule Trudel Bellemare

Pearson Australia
(a division of Pearson Australia Group Pty Ltd)
707 Collins Street, Melbourne, Victoria 3008
PO Box 23360, Melbourne, Victoria 8012
www.pearson.com.au

Printed under licence from Pearson Education Limited

Story by Dominic Barker
Illustrated by Paule Trudel Bellemare
Designed by Bigtop
First published 2011 by Pearson Education Limited
This edition published 2012 by Pearson Australia

2019 2018 2017 2016
10 9 8 7 6 5 4 3 2

ISBN 978 1 4425 5730 7

Printed in Australia by the SOS Print + Media Group

Pearson Australia Group Pty Ltd ABN 40 004 245 943

Acknowledgements
Every effort has been made to trace and acknowledge copyright. However, if any infringement has occurred, the publishers tender their apologies and invite the copyright holders to contact them.

CHAPTER 1

You Have *Got* To See This!

"I know you can curl your tongue," said Jack.

"And I know you *can't,*" said Shazia, curling her tongue for the five-hundredth time that day. "I've got a better tongue than you – *neh neh ne neh neh!*"

Shazia laughed.

Last week in school, Mr Brody, their teacher, had made everybody see if they could curl the edges of their tongue. Shazia could and Jack couldn't. She hadn't let him forget it.

"Let me get back to my game, Shaz," said Jack, picking up the controller.

"All right."

Shazia wandered over to the window. For a few moments, Jack's bedroom was filled with the sound of explosions and gunfire from his video game. Then …

"You have got to see this!" Shazia told him.

"Got to see what?"

Reluctantly, Jack dropped his controller and went to look out of the window.

All there was to see was a removal van parked over the road and a man and a boy carrying furniture and boxes out of it.

"That's you," said Shazia, nodding in the direction of the boy.

"Don't be sil–"

Jack ran out of words. He stared at his new neighbour. It couldn't be. Obviously it wasn't him. It was someone else.

But the someone else looked exactly like him.

"Let's go and say hello!" said Shazia.

CHAPTER 2

You Look Just Like Me!

"Are you sure this is a good idea?" asked Jack as Shazia knocked on the door.

"I only have good ideas," said Shazia.

The new boy answered. Close up, he looked even more like Jack.

"Hello," said Shazia, confidently. "I'm Shaz. This is Jack."

"So what?" said the boy, not even bothering to look at Jack.

"We live in the court," explained Shazia.

"And?" said the boy.

"So do you," said Shazia.

"The other side of town where we used to live is way better," said the boy. "At least I'm still going to the same school which I bet is better than *your* school."

The boy wasn't being very friendly. Jack decided maybe it was time to go.

"Come on, Shaz!" he said. "I don't think he wants ..."

For the first time, the boy looked at Jack. "Wow!" he said in surprise. "You look just like me."

"No," corrected Jack. "You look just like *me*!"

"Don't argue, boys!" said Shazia. "You look like each other." She turned to the new boy again. "So, what's your name?"

"I'm Oliver," he said, suddenly seeming more friendly.

"Okay, let's hang out!" said Shazia.

Jack sighed. When Shazia suggested they do something, they usually did it.

CHAPTER 3

I'm Not Scared!

They were sitting in the big tree in Shazia's backyard.

"We could dress exactly the same," suggested Jack. "People would think they were seeing double!"

"Boring," said Oliver. "I know! On Monday, we could pretend to be each other and go to each other's school and see if we can get through a day without getting found out!"

"Boring!" said Jack.

"That's not boring," said Shazia. "That's fantastic!"

Oliver gave Jack a smug look.

"It will be so funny in our school to see Oliver being you," said Shazia.

"But I don't want him to be me," protested Jack. "And I don't want to be him!"

"Why not?" said Oliver. "Don't you want to be popular for a day?"

Jack couldn't think of a clever reply fast enough.

"I just don't think that it's a good idea, that's all," said Jack.

"Unless you're scared?" asked Oliver, teasingly.

Jack was aware that Shazia was staring at him.

"Of course I'm not scared," said Jack.

"Prove it," said Oliver.

Jack was trapped.

"All right," he said. "I'll do it!"

CHAPTER 4

What Do You Think You Are Doing?

Jack's mobile beeped.

He clicked on it.

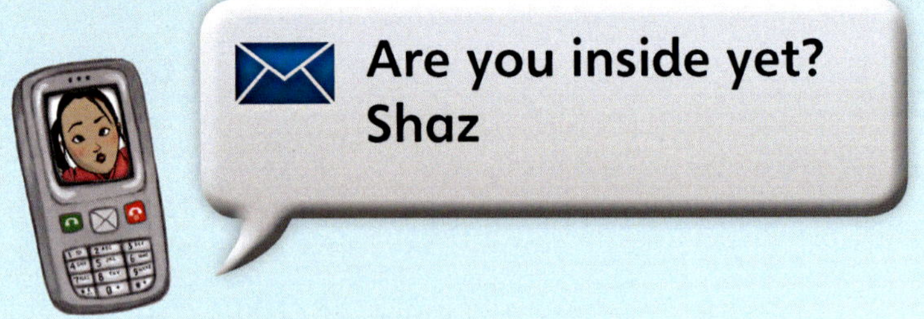

It was Monday. Jack was at the gates of Oliver's school, wishing he were anywhere else. He felt sure everybody could tell that he wasn't who he was pretending to be.

At least Oliver's uniform fitted him perfectly. They'd swapped in the shed in Shazia's backyard before setting off for each other's school.

Jack's mobile beeped again.

Everybody here thinks Oliver is you. Soooooo funny! Shaz

So Oliver had got away with it. Well, if Oliver could do it, thought Jack, then …

"Oliver Brandon!"

Jack looked up. A teacher was towering over him.

"What do you think you are doing?"

"I was just …" stammered Jack.

"Don't give me any of your cheek, young man," said the teacher. "Just get a move on. Don't talk. RUN."

He pointed in the direction of the classroom. Jack didn't have any choice. He ran.

CHAPTER 5

What's In Your Hand?

Oliver had told Jack that his place was at the table furthest from the teacher in the chair closest to the school guinea pig.

Jack sat there. He thought the other children were giving him funny looks. Could they tell?

A teacher swept into the room.

"Good morning, Miss Lynch," chorused the children.

"Good morning, class. How are–"

The teacher stopped in mid-sentence.

"Oliver Brandon. What do you think you are doing? After last week's incident with the guinea pig, your place is sitting next to my desk, as you well know. Move NOW, please."

With the eyes of the whole class on him, Jack stood up and walked to the front of the classroom and sat down at a table by the teacher's desk. Hoping maybe to find someone friendly, he smiled at the two girls sitting at the same table. They both totally ignored him.

Miss Lynch began to call the roll. As she was doing it, Jack spotted a $10 note on the floor. It must have fallen out of someone's bag. Maybe after getting off to such a bad start he could get back in Miss Lynch's good books by handing it in. He reached under the table and picked up the note.

"Miss Lynch! Miss Lynch! Miss Lynch!"

Jack looked up to see one of the girls who had ignored him with her hand in the air, staring right at him.

"What is it, Emily?"

"Oliver Brandon has Kelly Rowlands' money!"

Everyone looked at Jack.

"Is this true, Oliver?" asked Miss Lynch.

"It's in his hand, Miss!" cried Emily.

"Show me what's in your hand, Oliver."

Horrified, Jack did as he was told.

"That's my money!" cried Kelly. "I lost it this morning!"

"Oliver, I think you'd better go and explain this to Mr Henderson," said Miss Lynch.

"Who?" asked Jack.

"Don't pretend you don't know who Mr Henderson is," sighed Miss Lynch. "You spend more time outside his office than anywhere else."

CHAPTER 6

Are You Mr Henderson?

Jack gulped and knocked on the door. No answer. He took out his mobile and dialled Shazia's number. He had to know what was going on in his school.

No reply.

Of course. It was class time. Shazia wouldn't be able to answer. Jack wished more than anything that he was back in his school, in his classroom, sitting next to Shazia. But instead, Oliver was.

Jack texted Shazia.

"What do you think you are doing?"

Jack looked up.

The teacher from before was stomping down the corridor towards him.

"What did I tell you last week, Oliver?"

"Er … I'm not sure," Jack stuttered.

"Come on, young man, you must remember," thundered the teacher. "I told you quite clearly!"

"I can't," admitted Jack.

"I can't, *Mr Henderson*," said the teacher.

"Are *you* Mr Henderson?" asked Jack.

"Of course I'm Mr Henderson!" bellowed Mr Henderson. "I was Mr Henderson last week when you were sent to me! I was Mr Henderson the week before when you were sent to me! And I'm still Mr Henderson now!"

"Oh," said Jack. "Well that's good because there's been a terrible misunderstanding. You see–" Just then, his mobile beeped.

"And what's that in your hand?" demanded Mr Henderson.

Jack looked down.

"Er … a mobile."

"Hand it over, Oliver!"

Now Jack had no chance of finding out what was going on at his own school.

Mr Henderson looked irritated. "I hear you've been misbehaving again. Into my office – NOW!"

CHAPTER 7

This Has Gone Too Far!

In his office, Mr Henderson was busy listing examples of Oliver's past misbehaviour. There were so many that Jack was amazed that Oliver had found the time to fit in so much rule-breaking.

" ... then there was the flood in the boys' toilets," continued Mr Henderson. "And today – stealing! I'm going to phone your parents right now."

"This has gone too far," thought Jack. "I've got to tell him the truth."

Mr Henderson was picking up the phone on his desk.

"I'm not Oliver Brandon!" Jack said.

Mr Henderson hesitated.

"What did you say?"

"I'm not Oliver Brandon," repeated Jack. "I look like him but I'm not him. Oliver and I live near each other. We're swapping schools today for a joke."

Mr Henderson put the phone down and stared at Jack for a moment in silence.

"This has to be one of your best stories ever!" he said. "I suppose you can prove you aren't Oliver?"

"Of course I–" Jack stopped.

He was wearing Oliver's school uniform.

He'd brought Oliver's school bag filled with Oliver's books to school.

He looked exactly like Oliver.

He was trapped as Oliver!

Mr Henderson watched Jack squirm. "Well, I'm sure you can explain to your parents when they come to collect you that you aren't really their son!"

Before Mr Henderson could pick up the phone again, it rang.

"Oh, hello sir," he said.

It was obviously someone important. Mr Henderson swivelled his chair round so the back was towards Jack, and he carried on talking.

On Mr Henderson's desk, Jack's confiscated mobile beeped. Carefully, Jack reached for it and clicked on his inbox.

Jack knew that Oliver had done it before. That meant that he could do it again.

The back of Mr Henderson's chair was still towards him. Frantically, Jack sent a reply.

Mr Henderson was still on the phone. Jack stood up, tiptoed silently to the door, opened it … and ran!

CHAPTER 8

Bet You Can't Do This!

Jack ran the whole way from Oliver's school. More than three kilometres. He rushed through the school gates and found Shazia in the playground.

"I tried to stop him," said Shaz. "But he's gone to the one place in school I can't go – the boys' toilets!"

"Hey! What are you doing in this school?"

Jack and Shazia turned round.

Coming towards them was Mr Brody. For a moment, Jack couldn't work out why he was asking the question. But then he remembered – he was wearing the wrong school uniform! Mr Brody thought he was someone else. There was no time to explain …

"Come on, Shaz!" cried Jack.

They sprinted away from the teacher, zig-zagging through the crowded playground.

"Hey!" said Mr Brody, spilling his coffee as he began to give chase.

But Jack and Shazia kept going. Through the playground, into the main school building, down the corridor, past the Year 1 ... 2 ... 3 ... 4 ... 5 ... 6 classrooms and around the corner. There they were – the boys' toilets!

They charged into the toilets and came to a sudden stop. Oliver had already stuffed every plughole full of toilet paper and now he was running along the line of washbasins opening every tap as wide as it would go.

"Stop it!" shouted Jack.

Oliver spun round.

"What are you doing here?" he asked. "You were supposed to be me for the whole day."

"I've decided I want myself back. So stop this. Right now!"

Oliver shook his head.

"No way! This is fantastic! I get to be as naughty as I like and somebody else gets into trouble."

He reached the last tap and turned it on to full.

Already, the first basin was about to overflow. Jack rushed to turn it off.

Just as Jack's hand touched the tap, Mr Brody appeared, huffing and puffing.

"What on earth is going on here?"

Oliver got his words out first. "Mr Brody! This boy from another school is flooding the toilets!"

Mr Brody looked at Jack.

He was wearing the uniform of a different school and he had his hand on a tap.

"I was just going to come and tell you about it, Mr Brody," said Oliver.

The similarity of the two boys suddenly struck Mr Brody. Now he was very confused. He looked at Jack. Then he looked at Oliver. Then back at Jack. Then he made up his mind. "Shazia and Jack, I think you two had better return to class."

"And *you* need to explain what you are doing in this school, vandalising the toilets!" said Mr Brody to Jack.

Jack and Shazia looked at each other in horror. If Oliver got out of the toilets, he could run off and get away with everything and Jack would get all the blame.

With a smug smile, Oliver started to walk out of the toilets. As he passed Jack, he couldn't resist sticking his tongue out.

This gave Shazia an idea.

"Bet you can't do this," she said. She stuck out her tongue, curling it at the edges.

"Of course I can," said Oliver scornfully, and he curled the edges of his tongue.

"Mr Brody!" shouted Shazia. "Don't you remember in class last week? You asked us all to try that, and Jack was in the group that couldn't do it!"

Oliver started walking faster.

"You're right," remembered Mr Brody. "So that means …"

"That I'm the real Jack!" shouted Jack.

With a guilty look, Oliver darted for the door but Mr Brody cut off his escape.

"You, young man, have a lot of explaining to do."

After school, Jack and Shazia were sitting in the tree in her backyard.

"I like being me again," said Jack.

"You're better at being Jack than Oliver was," Shazia agreed.

"Do you think we'll be in a lot of trouble?"

"No," said Shazia. "Because, in the end, we *did* save the boys' toilets."

"Thanks to my rubbish tongue," said Jack.

He stuck out his tongue that still wouldn't curl.

"*Neh neh ne neh neh!*" said Shazia.

This time, they both laughed.